Contents

1. Introduction

- Definition, need, and types of programming languages and their selection criterion.
- Need for programming language. Computer programming languages: Machine language, assembly/low level language, middle-level language and high-level languages. Features and advantages and disadvantages.
- Algorithm and methods of writing algorithms: pseudo-code and flowcharts
- Features of pseudo-code or flow-charts
- Programming paradigms: Features of procedure oriented programming (POP) and object oriented programming (OOP) paradigms
- Program development process (writing, editing, compilation, linking, execution and debugging and file extensions) and tools
- Programming errors: Syntax, semantic, linker, and run-time (logical and data) errors
- C-program format
- Introduction to standard input and output statements
- Variables and constants: Definition, naming (identifiers or labels for different entities), initialization and accessing of variables. Constants and their representation
- Data types: classification, memory requirement, range of values, usage and type specifiers
- Operators and Operands: Unary, binary and ternary operators. Arithmetic, logical, relational, combinational-assignment and special operators. Precedence and associativity. Unary and binary operands
- Statements- tokens and expressions
- Type casting-automatic and forced
- Escape characters
- I/O statements in detail

2. Control structure

- Branching: Conditional (*if*, *if-else*, nested and ladder *if-else*, *switch* constructs) and unconditional (*brake*, *continue* and *goto* statements)
- Looping: Entry-controlled (*for* and *while*) and exit-controlled (*do while*) loops

3. Arrays/Matrices, strings and pointers

- Definition, declaration, initialization (static and run-time or dynamic) of arrays, strings and pointers
- Accessing of strings, arrays (one and two dimensional), and pointers

4. Functions

- Concept, pros and cons, classification, creation and application of functions
- Parameter passing: Pass by value and address methods
- Library and user-defined functions
- Recursive and non-recursive functions
- Data visibility and longevity

5. User-defined data-type

- Definition, declaration, initialization of members and variables of structures and unions
- Distinction between structures and unions
- Accessing of members of structures and unions

6. Macros

- Definition, classification and application of macros in program development

Chapter 1

Introduction

1.1 Programming Language

A programming language is a set of rules that provides a way of instructing the system to perform some operations.

A programming language in a formal constructed language designed to communicate instructions to a machine, particularly a computer is called Computer Programming Language

Hence programming languages can be used to create programs to control the behavior of a machine or to express algorithms. There are many programming languages: BASIC, COBOL, Pascal, FORTRAN, C, C++, JAVA are some examples.

1.2 Types of Programming languages

Programming languages are classified as:
- Machine language
- Assembly language
- High level language

1.2.1 Machine Language: The language of 0s and 1s is called as machine language. It is very tedious and error prone process of writing programs in machine languages. It is also called low level programming

Advantages
- Machine language makes fast and efficient use of the computer.
- It requires no translator to translate the code. It is directly understood by the computer.

Disadvantages
- All operation codes have to be remembered
- All memory addresses have to be remembered.
- It is hard to amend or find errors in a program written in the machine language.

1.2.2 Assembly Languages: It is advancement of low level programming language in which the sequence of 0s and 1s are replaced by mnemonic codes.

Example:- ADD for addition , SUB for subtraction etc

Since our system only understand the language of 0s and 1s, a system program known as **assembler** is designed to translate an assembly language program into the machine language program.

Advantages
- Assembly language is easier to understand and use as compared to machine language.
- It is easy to locate and correct errors.
- It is easily modified.

Disadvantages
- Like machine language, it is also machine dependent/specific.
- Since it is machine dependent, the programmer also needs to understand the hardware

1.2.3 High Level Language: High level languages are English like statements. Programs written in these languages are needed to be translated into machine language before to their execution using a system software **compiler.**

Some high level languages are **C, C++,** C#, JAVA, SQL, .NET etc

Advantages
- ☞ High-level languages are user-friendly
- ☞ They are similar to English and use English vocabulary and well-known symbols
- ☞ They are easier to learn
- ☞ They are easier to maintain
- ☞ They are problem-oriented rather than 'machine'-based
- ☞ A program written in a high-level language can be translated into many machine languages and can run on any computer for which there exists an appropriate translator
- ☞ The language is independent of the machine on which it is used i.e. programs developed in a high-level language can be run on any computer text

Disadvantages
- ☞ A high-level language has to be translated into the machine language by a translator, which takes up time
- ☞ The object code generated by a translator might be inefficient compared to an equivalent assembly language program

Points to remember
- ☞ Program written in high level languages are much easier to maintain and modify.
- ☞ High level language program is also called source code.
- ☞ Machine language program is also called object code.

1.3 Algorithm

In the context of computer programming, an algorithm, is defined as a: "well-ordered collection of unambiguous and effectively computable operations, that when executed, produces a result and halts in a finite amount of time."

1.3.1 Steps for Developing an Algorithm

The minimum steps to be followed in developing algorithm is as follows
1) Define the problem
2) List the inputs and the outputs
3) Describe the steps needed to convert or manipulate the inputs to produce the outputs
4) Test the algorithm

Methods of Writing Algorithms

There are two main methods of writing algorithms. They are
1) Pseudo code
2) Flowcharts

1.3.2 Pseudo Code

Pseudo code is a method of describing computer algorithms using a combination of natural language and programming language. It is essentially an intermittent step towards the development of the actual code. It allows the programmer to formulate their thoughts on the organization and sequence of a computer algorithm without the need for actually following the exact coding syntax. Although pseudo code is frequently used there are no set of rules for its exact implementation.

Features of Pseudo code
- ☞ Consists of natural language-like statements that precisely describe the steps of an algorithm or program

☞ Statements describe actions
☞ Focuses on the logic of the algorithm or program
☞ Avoids language-specific elements
☞ Written at a level so that the desired programming code can be generated almost automatically from each statement
☞ Steps are numbered. Subordinate numbers and/or indentation are used for dependent statements in selection and repetition structures.

1.3.3 Flow Charts

Flow charts are written with program flow from the top to the bottom. Each command is placed in a box of the appropriate shape, and arrows are used to direct program flow. The following shapes are often used in flowcharts:

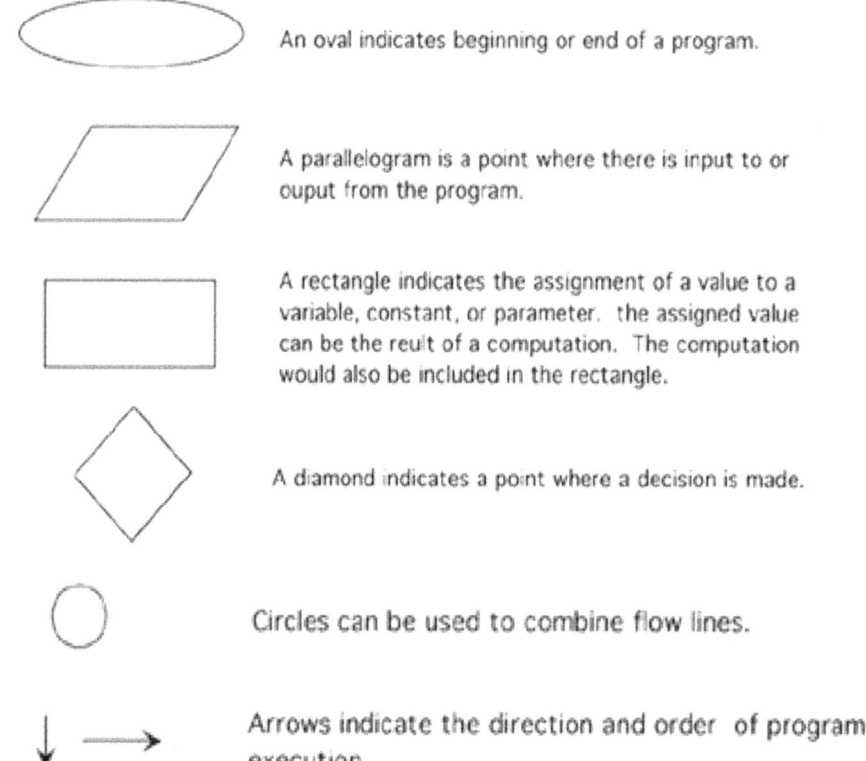

Features of flowcharts

☞ All symbols of the flowchart are connected by flow lines (arrows)
☞ Flow lines enter the top of the symbol and exit out the bottom, except for the Decision symbol, which can have flow lines exiting from the bottom or the sides
☞ Flowcharts are drawn so flow generally goes from top to bottom
☞ The beginning and the end of the flowchart is indicated using the Terminal symbol

1.4 Programming Paradigms

A paradigm is a style or "way" of programming. Some languages make it easy to write in some paradigms but not others. A programming paradigm is a fundamental style of computer programming, a way of building the structure and elements of computer programs. The main programming paradigms are as follows

1.4.1 Procedure-Oriented Programming

It is a type of programming where a structured method of creating programs is used. With procedure-oriented programming, a problem is broken up into parts and each part is then broken up into further parts. All these parts are known as procedures. They are separate but work together when needed. A main program centrally controls them all.

Some procedure-oriented languages are COBOL, FORTRAN, and C.

1.4.2 Object Oriented Programming

It is a type of programming where data types representing data structures are defined by the programmer as well as their properties and the things that can be done with them. With object-oriented programming, programmers can also create relationships between data structures and create new data types based on existing ones by having one data type inherit characteristics from another one.

In object-oriented programming, data types defined by the programmer are called classes (templates for a real world object to be used in a program). For example, a programmer can create a data type that represents a car - a car class. This class can contain the properties of a car (color, model, year, etc.) and functions that specify what the car does (drive, reverse, stop, etc.)

Some object-oriented languages include C++, Java, and PHP.

1.5 C Programming

C is a high-level structured oriented programming language, used in general purpose programming, developed by Dennis Ritchie at AT&T Bell labs, USA between 1969 and 1973.

☞ In 1988, C was formalized by American National Standard Institute (ANSI)
☞ C was invented to write UNIX operating system
☞ C is a successor of 'Basic Combined Programming Language' (BCPL) called B language
☞ Linux OS, PHP and MySQL is written in C
☞ C has been written in assembly language

1.5.1 Uses of C Language

In the beginning C was used for developing system applications e.g:

☞ Database Systems
☞ Language Interpreters
☞ Compilers and Assemblers
☞ Operating Systems
☞ Network Drivers
☞ Word Processors

1.5.2 Features of C Language

☞ It is a robust language with rich set of built-in functions and operators that can be used to write any complex program.
☞ The C compiler combines the capabilities of an assembly language with features of a high-level language.
☞ Programs Written in C are efficient and fast. This is due to its variety of data type and powerful operators.
☞ It is many time faster than BASIC.
☞ C is highly portable this means that programs once written can be run on another machines with little or no modification.
☞ Another important feature of C program, is its ability to extend itself.
☞ A C program is basically a collection of functions that are supported by C library. We can also create our own function and add it to C library.

☞ C language is the most widely used language in operating systems and embedded system development today.

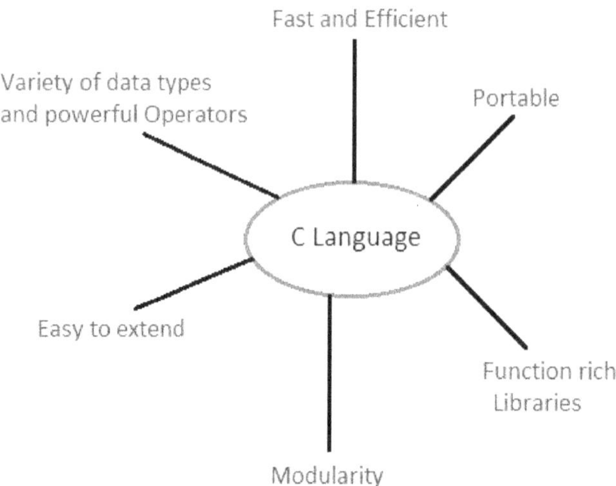

1.5.3 Some basic syntax rule for C program

☞ C is a case sensitive language so all C instructions must be written in lower case letter.

☞ All C statement must be end with a semicolon.

☞ Whitespace is used in C to describe blanks and tabs.

☞ Whitespace is required between keywords and identifiers

1.6 Program development process

There are many steps involved in converting a C program into an executable form, these all steps are called "build process". Build process are representing in the following graphically diagram:

C Source code Programs (assume file name filename.c)

Expanded source code (filename.i)

Assembly code (filename.asm)

Relocatable Object code + Object code of library function

Executable code (filename.exe)

If you don't understand the build process, don't worry, read following explanations of build process i.e. how a source program make executable program. It is all internal process of machine, that's done in nano seconds. Lets now understand the steps mentioned in above figure in detail.

Editor: Type your program in editor (source code).

Preprocessing: During this step, the C source code is expanded based on the preprocessor directives like as **#include**, **#ifdef**, **#define** etc. The expanded source code is stored in an intermediate file with .i extension.

Compilation: The expanded source code is then passed to the compiler, which identifies the syntax error in the expanded source code. If the expanded source code is error free, then the compiler transfer the expanded source code in C, into an equivalent assembly language program. The assembly code is typically stored in .ASM file. So our filename.C file would be changed and stored in filename.ASM.

Assembling: Assembler translate the .ASM program into Re-locatable Object code. Thus assembler translates our filename.asm file into filename.OBJ. .OBJ file is one of the binary file. This object file contained header and several sections.

Linking: Linking is the final step of build process i.e., creating an executable program. It does following works:
> ☞ Find definition of all external function
> ☞ Find definition of all global variables
> ☞ Combine Data Section
> ☞ Combine Code Section

Loading - Once the .EXE file is created and stored on the disk, it is ready for execution. when we execute it, it is first brought from the disk into the memory (RAM) by an OS component called Program Loader.

Execution: The executable file is a file with .exe extension. This is the final running version of the program (in language which the computer understands). When this file is executed, the output is produced.

1.6.1 Programming Errors

Due to certain mistake, the execution of program will be stopped or can give wrong result. This mistake is called programming error. It is identified by debugging.

Debugging: There is a possibility of occurrence of errors in programs. These errors must be removed to ensure proper working of programs. Hence error check is made. This process is known as "Debugging".

Types of errors that may occur in the program are:
☞ Syntax error
☞ Logical error
☞ Logical error
☞ Runtime error

Syntax error: This error occurs due to mistake in writing the syntax of a c statement or wrong use of reserved words, improper variable names, using variables without declaration etc.

Examples are : missing semi colon or paranthesis, type integer for int datatype etc.

Appropriate error message and the statement number will be displayed. You can see the statement and make correction to the program file, save and recompile it.

Logical error: This error occurs due to the flaw in the logic. This will not be identified by the compiler. However it can be traced using the debug tool in the editor.

Linker error: This error occur when the files during linking are missing or misspell

Runtime error: This error occurs if the program encounters division by zero, accessing a null pointer etc during execution of the program.

1.6.2 C Compile and Run Steps

There are many different ways to compile and run a C program. All that is required is a C compiler. We will recommend you to use **turbo c** IDE, oldest IDE for c programming. It is freely available over internet and is good for a beginner.

Step 1: Open turbo C IDE (Integrated Development Environment), click on **File** and then click on New

Step 2: Write the program code in the editor

Step 3: Click on compile or press Alt+f9 to compile the code

Step 4: Click on Run or press Ctrl+f9 to run the code

Step 5: Output window will open

1.7 C-Program Format

The different parts of C program are.

- ☞ Pre-processor
- ☞ Header file
- ☞ Function
- ☞ Variables
- ☞ expression
- ☞ Comment etc

All these are essential parts of a C language program.

The simple syntax of C program is as below

```
#include<stdio.h>
int main()
{
 int i ;
 // Asking user for value
 printf("Enter a value") ;
 scanf("%d", &i) ;
 getch() ;
 return 0;
}
```

Let's look into various parts of the above C program.

/* Comments */: Comments are a way of explaining what makes a program. Comments are ignored by the compiler and used by others to understand the code.

#include<stdio.h>: stdio is standard for input / output, this allows us to use some commands which includes a file called stdio.h.

main(): The main() is the main function where program execution begins. Every C program must contain only one main function.

Braces Two curly brackets "{...}" are used to group all statements together.

Printf(): It is a function in C, which prints text on the screen.

Scanf() and getch(): It is a function in C, which takes input from keyboard

return 0: At the end of the main function returns value 0.

1.8 Standard Input and Output statements

C programming has several in-build library functions to perform input and output tasks. Two commonly used functions for I/O (Input/Output) are printf() and scanf().

The scanf() function reads formatted input from standard input (keyboard) whereas the printf() function sends formatted output to the standard output (screen).

The **format** can be a simple constant string, but you can specify %s, %d, %c, %f, etc., to print or read strings, integer, character or float respectively. There are many other formatting options available which can be used based on requirements. Let us now proceed with a simple example to understand the concepts better

```c
#include <stdio.h>
int main( ) {

    char str[100];
    int i;

    printf( "Enter a value :");
    scanf("%s %d", str, &i);

    printf( "\nYou entered: %s %d ", str, i);

    return 0;
}
```

When the above code is compiled and executed, it waits for you to input some text. When you enter a text and press enter, then program proceeds and reads the input and displays it as follows

```
Enter a value : seven 7
You entered: seven 7
```

Here, it should be noted that scanf() expects input in the same format as you provided %s and %d, which means you have to provide valid inputs like "string for %s and integer for %d".

1.9 Keywords

Keywords are preserved words that have special meaning in C language. The meaning has already been described. These meaning cannot be changed. There are total 32 keywords in C language.

auto	double	int	struct
break	else	long	switch
case	enum	register	typedef
const	extern	return	union
char	float	short	unsigned
continue	for	signed	volatile
default	goto	sizeof	void
do	if	static	while

1.10 Identifiers

In C language identifiers are the names given to variables, constants, functions and user-define data. These identifier are defined against a set of rules.

1.10.1 Rules for an Identifier

1. An identifier can only have alphanumeric characters(a-z , A-Z , 0-9) and underscore(_).
2. The first character of an identifier can only contain alphabet(a-z , A-Z) or underscore (_).
3. Identifiers are also case sensitive in C. For example name and Name are two different identifier in C.
4. Keywords are not allowed to be used as Identifiers.
5. No special characters, such as semicolon, period, whitespaces, slash or comma are permitted to be used in or as Identifier.

1.11 Variables

A variable is a name that may be used to store a data value. Unlike constant, variables are changeable, we can change value of a variable during execution of a program. A programmer can choose a meaningful variable name. Example : average, height, age, total etc.

1.11.1 Rules to define variable name

☞ Variable name must be upto 8 characters.
☞ Variable name must not start with a digit.
☞ Variable name can consist of alphabets, digits and special symbols like underscore _.
☞ Blank or spaces are not allowed in variable name.
☞ Keywords are not allowed as variable name.

1.11.2 Declaration of variable

Declaration of variables must be done before they are used in the program.

        type variable_name;

        or

        type variable_name, variable_name, variable_name;

Declaration does two things.

1. It tells the compiler what the variable name is.
2. It specifies what type of data the variable will hold.

```c
#include<stdio.h>
#include<conio.h>
```

```
void main()
{
 int a,b,sum;      //variable declaraction
 a=10;
 b=20;
 sum=a+b;
 printf("Sum is %d",sum);
 getch();
}
```

1.12 Constants

Constants are like variable, except that their value never changes during execution once defined.

☞ Constants are also called literals.
☞ Constants can be any of the data type.
☞ It is considered best practice to define constants using only upper-case names.

1.12.1 Constant declaration in C

```
const type constant_name;
```
Example:
```
#include<stdio.h>
main()
{
const int SIDE = 10;
int area;
area = SIDE*SIDE;
printf("The area of the square with side: %d is: %d sq. units"
, SIDE, area);
}
```

It is possible to put const either before or after the type.
```
int const SIDE = 10;
or
const int SIDE = 10;
```

1.13 Data types in C Language

Data types specify how we enter data into our programs and what type of data we enter. C language has some predefined set of data types to handle various kinds of data that we use in our program. These data types have different storage capacities.

C language supports 2 different types of data types,

Primary data types: These are fundamental data types in C namely integer (int), floating (float), character (char) and void.

Derived data types: Derived data types are like arrays, functions, structures and pointers. These are discussed in detail later.

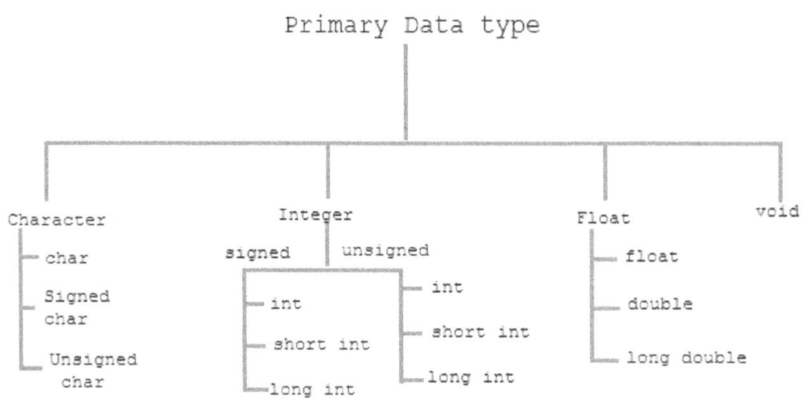

Integer type: Integers are used to store whole numbers. Size and range of Integer type on 16-bit machine is given in the below table

Type	Size(bytes)	Range
int or signed int	2	-32,768 to 32767
unsigned int	2	0 to 65535
short int or signed short int	1	-128 to 127
long int or signed long int	4	-2,147,483,648 to 2,147,483,647
unsigned long int	4	0 to 4,294,967,295

Floating type: Floating types are used to store real numbers. Size and range of Integer type on 16-bit machine is given in the below table

Type	Size(bytes)	Range
Float	4	3.4E-38 to 3.4E+38
double	8	1.7E-308 to 1.7E+308
long double	10	3.4E-4932 to 1.1E+4932

Character type: Character types are used to store characters value. Size and range of Integer type on 16-bit machine is given in the below table

Type	Size(bytes)	Range
char or signed char	1	-128 to 127
unsigned char	1	0 to 255

Void type: Void type means no value. This is usually used to specify the type of functions.

1.14 Operators in C Language

C language supports a rich set of built-in operators. An operator is a symbol that tells the compiler to perform certain mathematical or logical manipulations. Operators are used in program to manipulate data and variables.

C operators can be classified into following types,

☞ Arithmetic operators
☞ Relation operators
☞ Logical operators

☞ Bitwise operators
☞ Assignment operators
☞ Conditional operators
☞ Special operators

1.14.1 Arithmetic Operators

C supports all the basic arithmetic operators. The following table shows all the basic arithmetic operators.

Operator	Description
+	adds two operands
-	subtract second operands from first
*	multiply two operand
/	divide numerator by denumerator
%	remainder of division
++	Increment operator increases integer value by one
--	Decrement operator decreases integer value by one

1.14.2 Relation Operators

The following table shows all relation operators supported by C.

Operator	Description
==	Check if two operand are equal
!=	Check if two operand are not equal.
>	Check if operand on the left is greater than operand on the right
<	Check operand on the left is smaller than right operand
>=	check left operand is greater than or equal to right operand
<=	Check if operand on left is smaller than or equal to right operand

1.14.3 Logical Operators

C language supports following 3 logical operators. Suppose a=1 and b=0,

Operator	Description	Example
&&	Logical AND	(a && b) is false
||	Logical OR	(a || b) is true
!	Logical NOT	(!a) is false

1.14.4 Bitwise Operators

Bitwise operators perform manipulations of data at bit level. These operators also perform shifting of bits from right to left. Bitwise operators are not applied to float or double.

Operator	Description
&	Bitwise AND
|	Bitwise OR
^	Bitwise exclusive OR
<<	left shift

>>	right shift

Now lets see truth table for bitwise &, | and ^

a	b	a & b	a | b	a ^ b
0	0	0	0	0
0	1	0	1	1
1	0	0	1	1
1	1	1	1	0

The bitwise shift operators shifts the bit value. The left operand specifies the value to be shifted and the right operand specifies the number of positions that the bits in the value are to be shifted. Both operands have the same precedence.

Example :

```
a = 0001000
b= 2
a << b = 0100000
a >> b = 0000010
```

1.14.5 Assignment Operators

Assignment operators supported by C language are as follows.

Operator	Description	Example
=	assigns values from right side operands to left side operand	a=b
+=	adds right operand to the left operand and assign the result to left	a+=b is same as a=a+b
-=	subtracts right operand from the left operand and assign the result to left operand	a-=b is same as a=a-b
*=	mutiply left operand with the right operand and assign the result to left operand	a*=b is same as a=a*b
/=	divides left operand with the right operand and assign the result to left operand	a/=b is same as a=a/b
%=	calculate modulus using two operands and assign the result to left operand	a%=b is same as a=a%b

1.14.6 Conditional Operator

It is also known as ternary operator and used to evaluate conditional expression.

```
epr1 ? expr2 : expr3
```

If epr1 Condition is true ? Then value expr2 : Otherwise value expr3

1.14.7 Special Operator

Operator	Description	Example
sizeof	Returns the size of an variable	**sizeof(x)** return size of the variable **x**
&	Returns the address of an variable	**&x ;** return address of the variable **x**

*	Pointer to a variable	***x** ; will be pointer to a variable **x**

1.14.8 Type-Cast Operator

The type cast operator is very important in C. Cast operator uses in convert one data type to another data types. Type casting may be two types:

1. Implicit type cast
2. Explicit type cast

Implicit Type Cast

In C, implicit type cast are automatically handled by compiler i.e. when two or more data types are getting execution then the final data-type will be that data type as it is declared, i.e it is not depend on conversion of data type.

It is clear understand by example as:

```c
#include<stdio.h>
#include<conio.h>
void main()
{
  int i,j;
  float f;
  double d;
  i=d*f+f*j;
}
```

what you think, what will be data type of i? it is double!! No, right answer is int. You see in program that double has high priority or precedence of float and int, so result of data type will be comes in double but when result is assign in i, it will be convert in int because i is declared as int. It is implicit type casting.

Explicit Type Cast

An explicit type cast is a cast that we should specify invoke with either the cast. The compiler does not automatically invoke to resolve the data type conversion.

Let's understand explicit with example:

```c
/*A student marks of three subject as m1,m2,m3 and calculate percentage(per)*/
#include<stdio.h>
#include<conio.h>
void main()
{
  int m1=70,m2=70,m3=100,total;
  float per;
  total=m1+m2+m3;
  per=total/300*100;
  printf("%f",per);
}
```

output:- 0.000000

Look at per=total/300*100; statement. In this statement first of all total/300 will be solve so total(240) and 300 are int hence 240/300 will be produce a float value so result is 0.000000.

1.14.9 Operators Precedence

Operator precedence determines the grouping of terms in an expression and decides how an expression is evaluated. Certain operators have higher precedence than others; for example, the multiplication operator has a higher precedence than the addition operator.

For example, x = 7 + 3 * 2; here, x is assigned 13, not 20 because operator * has a higher precedence than +, so it first gets multiplied with 3*2 and then adds into 7.

Here, operators with the highest precedence appear at the top of the table, those with the lowest appear at the bottom. Within an expression, higher precedence operators will be evaluated first.

Category	Operator	Associativity
Postfix	() [] -> . ++ - -	Left to right
Unary	+ - ! ~ ++ - - (type)* & sizeof	Right to left
Multiplicative	* / %	Left to right
Additive	+ -	Left to right
Shift	<< >>	Left to right
Relational	< <= > >=	Left to right
Equality	== !=	Left to right
Bitwise AND	&	Left to right
Bitwise XOR	^	Left to right
Bitwise OR	|	Left to right
Logical AND	&&	Left to right
Logical OR	||	Left to right
Conditional	?:	Right to left
Assignment	= += -= *= /= %=>>= <<= &= ^= |=	Right to left

1.15 Input Output Function in detail

C programming language provides many of the built-in functions to read given input and write data on screen, printer or in any file.

1.15.1 scanf() and printf() functions
Note scanf() and printf() functions are already explained in section 1.8

1.15.2 getchar() & putchar() functions

The getchar() function reads a character from the terminal and returns it as an integer. This function reads only single character at a time. You can use this method in the loop in case you want to read more than one characters.

The putchar() function prints the character passed to it on the screen and returns the same character. This function puts only single character at a time. In case you want to display more than one characters, use putchar() method in the loop.

Example

```c
#include <stdio.h>
#include <conio.h>
void main ( )
{
  int c;
  printf("Enter a character");
  c=getchar();
  putchar(c);
  getch();
}
```

When you will compile the above code, it will ask you to enter a value. When you will enter the value, it will display the value you have entered.

1.15.3 gets() & puts() functions

The gets() function reads a line from **stdin** into the buffer pointed to by **s** until either a terminating newline or EOF (end of file). The puts() function writes the string **s** and a trailing newline to stdout.

Example: C program to read and display the string using gets() and put() functions

```c
#include<stdio.h>
#include<conio.h>
void main()
{
  char str[100];
  printf("Enter a string");
  gets( str );
  puts( str );
  getch();
}
```

When you will compile the above code, it will ask you to enter a string. When you will enter the string, it will display the value you have entered.

1.15.4 Difference between scanf() and gets()

The main difference between these two functions is that scanf() stops reading characters when it encounters a space, but gets() reads space as character too.

If you enter name as GPT GADAG using scanf() it will only read and store GPT and will leave the part after space. But gets() function will read it complete.

Chapter 2

Control Structure

2.1 Branching/Decision making in C

Decision making is about deciding the order of execution of statements based on certain conditions or repeat a group of statements until certain specified conditions are met. C language handles decision-making by supporting the following statements,

- ☞ if statement
- ☞ switch statement
- ☞ conditional operator statement
- ☞ goto statement

2.2 Decision making with "if" statement

The "if" statement may be implemented in different forms depending on the complexity of conditions to be tested. The different forms are of "if" statements are,

1. Simple if statement
2. If....else statement
3. Nested if....else statement
4. else if statement

2.2.1 Simple if statement

The general form of a simple if statement is,

```
If(expression)
{
 statement-inside;
}
 statement-outside;
```

If the expression is true, then 'statement-inside' will be executed, otherwise 'statement-inside' is skipped and only 'statement-outside' is executed.

Example: C program to find the largest of 2 numbers using "if" statement

```
#include <stdio.h>
void main( )
{
 int x,y;
 x=15;
 y=13;
 if (x > y )
 {
```

```
  printf("x is greater than y");
 }
}
```
output: x is greater than y

2.2.2 if...else statement
The general form of a simple if...else statement is,
```
if(expression)
{
 statement-block1;
}
else
{
 statement-block2;
}
```

If the 'expression' is true, the 'statement-block1' is executed, else 'statement-block1' is skipped and 'statement-block2' is executed.

Example: C program to find the largest of 2 numbers using if-else statement
```
#include <stdio.h>
void main( )
{
 int x,y;
 x=15;
 y=18;
 if (x > y )
 {
  printf("x is greater than y");
 }
 else
 {
  printf("y is greater than x");
 }
}
```
Output:
y is greater than x

2.2.3 Nested if....else statement
The general form of a nested if...else statement is,
```
if( expression )
{
  if( expression1 )
   {
     statement-block1;
   }
```

```c
else
  {
    statement-block 2;
  }
}
else
{
 statement-block 3;
}
```

If 'expression' is false the 'statement-block3' will be executed, otherwise it continues to perform the test for 'expression 1'. If the 'expression 1' is true the 'statement-block1' is executed otherwise 'statement-block2' is executed.

Example: C program to find the largest of 3 numbers using nested if-else statement

```c
#include <stdio.h>
#include <conio.h>
void main( )
{
 int a,b,c;
 clrscr();
 printf("enter 3 number");
 scanf("%d%d%d",&a,&b,&c);
 if(a>b)
 {
  if( a > c)
  {
    printf("a is greatest");
  }
  else
  {
    printf("c is greatest");
  }
 }
 else
 {
  if( b> c)
   {
    printf("b is greatest");
   }
  else
   {
    printf("c is greatest");
   }
 }
getch();
```

```
}
```

2.2.4 else-if Ladder

The general form of else-if ladder is,

```
if(expression 1)
{
 statement-block1;
}
else if(expression 2)
{
 statement-block2;
}
else if(expression 3 )
{
 statement-block3;
}
else
 default-statement;
```

The expression is tested from the top (of the ladder) downwards. As soon as the true condition is found, the statement associated with it is executed.

Example: C program to find the the entered number is divisible by 5 or 8 or by both or none using else-if ladder statement

```
#include <stdio.h>
#include <conio.h>
void main( )
{
 int a;
 printf("enter a number");
 scanf("%d",&a);
 if( a%5==0 && a%8==0)
 {
  printf("divisible by both 5 and 8");
 }
 else if( a%8==0 )
 {
  printf("divisible by 8");
 }
 else if(a%5==0)
 {
  printf("divisible by 5");
 }
 else
 {
  printf("divisible by none");
```

```
  }
getch();
}
```

Points to Remember

1. In if statement, a single statement can be included without enclosing it into curly braces { }

   int a = 5;

   if(a > 4)

     printf("success");

   No curly braces are required in the above case, but if we have more than one statement inside if condition, then we must enclose them inside curly braces.

2. "==" must be used for comparison in the expression of "if condition", if you use "=" the expression will always return true, because it performs assignment not comparison.

3. Other than **0(zero)**, all other values are considered as true.

   if(27)

   printf("hello");

   In above example, hello will be printed.

2.3 Switch Statement

Switch statement is used to solve multiple option type problems for menu like program, where one value is associated with each option. The **expression** in switch case evaluates to return an integral value, which is then compared to the values in different cases, where it matches that block of code is executed, if there is no match, then default block is executed. The general form of **switch** statement is,

```
switch(expression)
{
 case value-1:
      block-1;
      break;
 case value-2:
      block-2;
      break;
 case value-3:
      block-3;
      break;
 case value-4:
      block-4;
      break;
 default:
      default-block;
      break;
}
```

Points to Remember

1. We don't use those expressions to evaluate switch case, which may return floating point values or strings.

2. It isn't necessary to use **break** after each block, but if you do not use it, all the consecutive block of codes will get executed after the matching block.

```c
int i = 1;
switch(i)
{
  case 1:
    printf("A");          // No break
  case 2:
    printf("B");          // No break
  case 3:
    printf("C");
    break;
}
Output: A B C
```

The output was supposed to be only **A** because only the first case matches, but as there is no break statement after the block, the next blocks are executed, until the cursor encounters a break.

3. **Default** case can be placed anywhere in the switch case. Even if we don't include the default case switch statement works.

Example: C program to use as calculator for addition and subtraction operations using switch statement

```c
#include<stdio.h>
#include<conio.h>
void main( )
 {
  int a,b,c,choice;
  clrscr( );
  while(choice!=3)
  {
   printf("\n 1. Press 1 for addition");
   printf("\n 2. Press 2 for subtraction");
   printf("\n Enter your choice");
   scanf("%d", &choice);
   switch(choice)
   {
    case 1:
      printf("Enter 2 numbers");
      scanf("%d%d",&a,&b);
      c=a+b;
      printf("%d",c);
      break;
    case 2:
      printf("Enter 2 numbers");
      scanf("%d%d",&a,&b);
      c=a-b;
      printf("%d",c);
```

```
    break;
  default:
    printf("you have passed a wrong key");
    printf("\n press any key to continue");

    }
  }
 getch();
}
```

2.4.1 How to use Loops in C Language

In any programming language, loops are used to execute a set of statements repeatedly until a particular condition is satisfied.

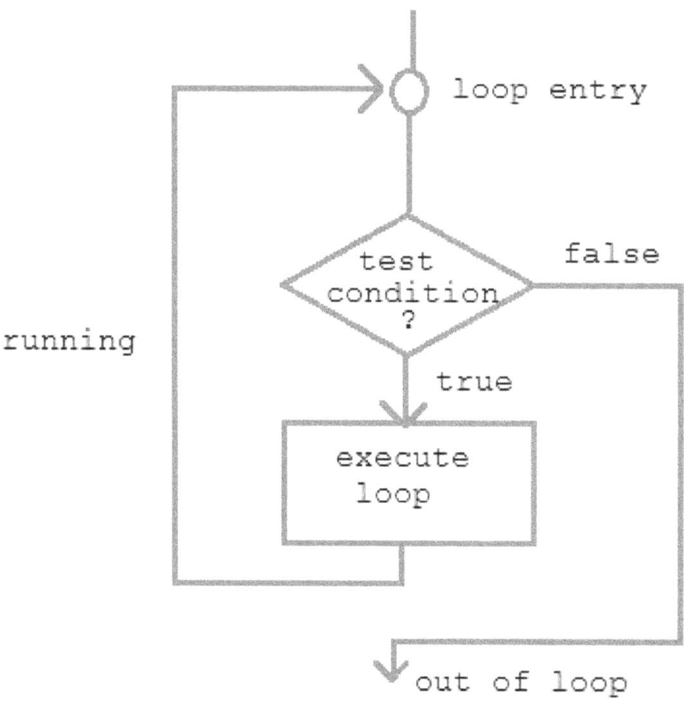

A sequence of statements are executed until a specified condition is true. This sequence of statements to be executed is kept inside the curly braces { } known as the loop body. After every execution of loop body, condition is verified, and if it is found to be true the loop body is executed again. When the condition check returns false, the loop body is not executed.

2.4.2 Types of Loops

There are 3 type of Loops in C language

☞ while loop

☞ for loop

☞ do-while loop

2.4.3 While loop

While loop can be addressed as an entry control loop. It is completed in 3 steps.

☞ Variable initialization.(e.g int x=0;)

☞ Condition check (e.g while(x<=10))
☞ Variable increment or decrement (x++ or x-- or x=x+2)

Syntax:
```
variable initialization ;
while (condition)
{
 statements ;
 variable increment or decrement ;
}
```

Example: Program to print first 10 natural numbers using while loop
```
#include<stdio.h>
#include<conio.h>
void main( )
{
 int x;
 x=1;
 while(x<=10)
 {
   printf("%d\t", x);
   x++;
 }
 getch();
}
output
1 2 3 4 5 6 7 8 9 10
```

2.4.4 for loop

"for" loop is used to execute a set of statements repeatedly until a particular condition is satisfied. We can say it an open ended loop. General format is,
```
for(initialization; condition ; increment/decrement)
{
   statement-block;
}
```

In "for" loop we have exactly two semicolons, one after initialization and second after condition. In this loop we can have more than one initialization or increment/decrement, separated using comma operator. "for" loop can have only one condition.

Example: Program to print first 10 natural numbers using for loop
```
#include<stdio.h>
#include<conio.h>
void main( )
{
 int x;
```

```c
for(x=1; x<=10; x++)
{
   printf("%d\t",x);
}
getch();
}
```

Output

```
1 2 3 4 5 6 7 8 9 10
```

Nested for loop

We can also have nested **for** loops, i.e one **for** loop inside another **for** loop. Basic syntax is,

```c
for(initialization; condition; increment/decrement)
{
   for(initialization; condition; increment/decrement)
   {
      statement ;
   }
}
```

Example: Program to print half Pyramid of numbers

```c
#include<stdio.h>
#include<conio.h>
void main( )
{
 int i,j;
 for(i=1;i<5;i++)
 {
   printf("\n");
   for(j=i;j>0;j--)
   {
     printf("%d",j);
   }
 }
 getch();
}
```

output

```
1
21
321
4321
54321
```

2.4.5 do while loop

In some situations it is necessary to execute body of the loop before testing the condition. Such situations can be handled with the help of **do-while** loop. **do** statement evaluates the body of the loop first and at the end, the condition is checked using **while** statement. General format of **do-while** loop is,

```
do
{
 ....
 .....
}
while(condition)
```

Example: Program to print first ten multiple of 5 using do while loop.

```
#include<stdio.h>
#include<conio.h>
void main()
{
  int a,i;
  a=5;
  i=1;
  do
  {
    printf("%d\t",a*i);
    i++;
  }
  while(i <= 10);
getch();
}
output
5 10 15 20 25 30 35 40 45 50
```

2.5 Jumping Out of Loops

Sometimes, while executing a loop, it becomes necessary to skip a part of the loop or to leave the loop as soon as certain condition becomes true, that is called jumping out of loop. C language allows jumping from one statement to another within a loop as well as jumping out of the loop.

break statement: When break statement is encountered inside a loop, the loop is immediately exited and the program continues with the statement immediately following the loop.

```
while( condition check )
{
    statement-1;
    statement-2;
    if( some condition)
    {
        break;
    }
    statement-3;
    statement-4;
}
        Jumps out of the loop, no matter how
        many cycles are left, loop is exited.
```

continue statement: It causes the control to go directly to the test-condition and then continue the loop process. On encountering continue, cursor leave the current cycle of loop, and starts with the next cycle.

```
while( condition check )
{
    statement-1;
    statement-2;
    if( some condition)
    {
        continue;
    }
    statement-3;
    statement-4;
}
```

Jumps to the next cycle directly.

Not executed for the cycle of loop in which continue is executed.

goto statement: Transfers control to the labeled statement.

Chapter 3
Arrays/Matrices, strings and pointers

3.1 Arrays

In C language, arrays are referred to as structured data types. An array is defined as finite ordered collection of homogenous data, stored in contiguous memory locations.

Here the words,
☞ finite means data range must be defined.
☞ ordered means data must be stored in continuous memory addresses.
☞ homogenous means data must be of similar data type.

Example where arrays are used,
☞ to store list of Employee or Student names,
☞ to store marks of a students,
☞ to store list of numbers or characters etc.

Since arrays provide an easy way to represent data, it is classified amongst the data structures in C. Other data structures in c are structure, lists, queues and trees. Array can be used to represent not only simple list of data but also table of data in two or three dimensions.

3.1.1 Declaring an Array

Like any other variable, arrays must be declared before they are used. General form of array declaration is,

```
data-type variable-name[size];
```

Example:

```
int arr[10];
```

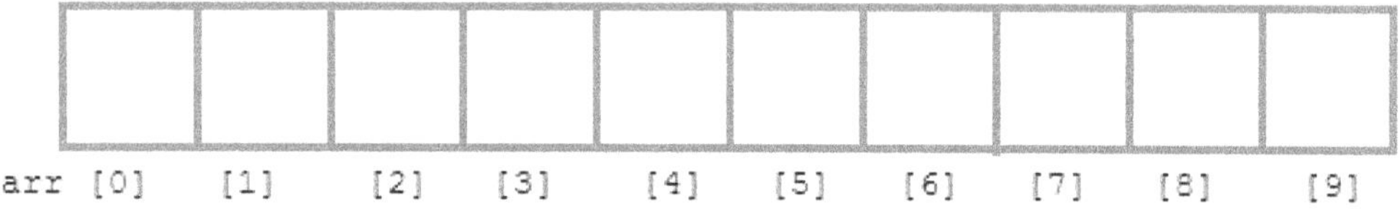

Here `int` is the data type, `arr` is the name of the array and 10 is the size of array. It means array arr can only contain 10 elements of int type. Index of an array starts from 0 to size-1 i.e first element of arr array will be stored at arr[0] address and last element will occupy arr[9].

3.1.2 Initialization of an Array

After an array is declared it must be initialized. Otherwise, it will contain garbage value (any random value). An array can be initialized at either compile time or at runtime.

3.1.3 Compile time Array Initialization

Compile time initialization of array elements is same as ordinary variable initialization. The general form of initialization of array is,

```
type array-name[size] = { list of values };
```

Examples:

```
int marks[4]={ 67, 87, 56, 77 }; //integer array initialization
float area[5]={ 23.4, 6.8, 5.5 }; //float array initialization
int marks[4]={ 67, 87, 56, 77, 59 };  //Compile time error
```

One important thing to remember is that when you will give more initializer than, declared array size than, the compiler will give an error.

Example: Program to display the elements using compile time array initialization.

```c
#include<stdio.h
#include<conio.h>
void main()
{
 int i;
 int arr[]={2,3,4};     //Compile time array initialization
 for(i=0 ; i<3 ; i++) {
    printf("%d\t",arr[i]);
 }
 getch();
}
```

Output: 2 3 4

3.1.4 Runtime Array initialization

An array can also be initialized at runtime using scanf() function. This approach is usually used for initializing large array, or to initialize array with user specified values. Example,

Example: Program to read and display the elements using run time array initialization.

```c
#include<stdio.h>
#include<conio.h>
void main()
{
 int arr[4];
 int i, j;
 printf("Enter array element");
 for(i=0;i<4;i++)
 {
  scanf("%d",&arr[i]);     //Run time array initialization
 }
 for(j=0;j<4;j++)
 {
  printf("%d\n",arr[j]);
 }
 getch();
}
```

3.1.5 Two dimensional Arrays

C language supports multidimensional arrays. The simplest form of the multidimensional array is the two-dimensional array. Two-dimensional array is declared as follows,

```c
type array-name[row-size][column-size]
```

Example :

```c
int a[3][4];
```

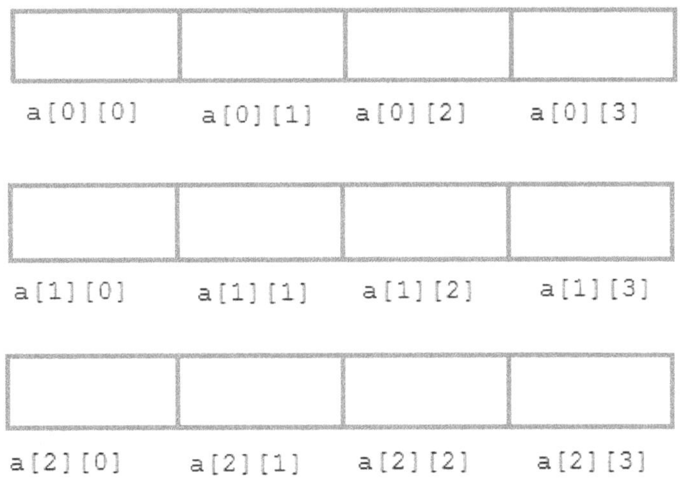

The above array can also be declared and initialized together. Such as,

```c
int arr[][3] = {
            {0,0,0},
            {1,1,1}
            };
```

Example: Program to read and display the elements of 3X4 matrix using two dimensional array.

```c
#include<stdio.h>
#include<conio.h>
void main()
{
 int arr[3][4];
 int i,j,k;
 printf("Enter array element");
 for(i=0;i<3;i++)
 {
  for(j=0; j < 4; j++)
  {
   scanf("%d",&arr[i][j]);
  }
 }
 for(i=0; i < 3; i++)
 {
  for(j=0; j < 4; j++)
  {
   printf("%d",arr[i][j]);
  }
 }
getch();
}
```

3.2 String and Character array

String is a sequence of characters that is treated as a single data item and terminated by null character '\0'. Remember that C language does not support strings as a data type. A string is actually one-dimensional array of characters in C language. These are often used to create meaningful and readable programs.

For example: The string "GPT Gadag" contains 10 characters including '\0' character which is automatically added by the compiler at the end of the string.

3.2.1 Declaring and Initializing a String Variables

There are different ways to initialize a character array variable.

```c
char name[10]="StudyTonight"; //valid character array initialization

char name[10]={'v','a','g','g','a','\0'}; //valid initialization
```

Remember that when you initialize a character array by listings all its characters separately then you must supply the '\0' character explicitly.

3.2.2 String Input and Output

Input function scanf() can be used with **%s** format specifier to read a string input from the terminal. But there is one problem with **scanf()** function, it terminates its input on first white space it encounters. Therefore if you try to read an input string "GPT Gadag" using **scanf()** function, it will only read GPT and terminate after encountering white spaces.

However, C supports a format specification known as the **edit set conversion code %[..]** that can be used to read a line containing a variety of characters, including white spaces.

```c
#include<stdio.h>
#include<conio.h>
#include<string.h>
void main()
{
 char str[20];
 clrscr();
 printf("Enter a string");
 scanf("%[^\n]",&str);
 printf("%s",str);
 getch();
}
```

Another method to read character string with white spaces from terminal is **gets()** function.

```c
char text[20];
gets(text);
printf("%s",text);
```

3.2.3 String Handling Functions

C language supports a large number of string handling functions that can be used to carry out many of the string manipulations. These functions are packaged in **string.h** library. Hence, you must include **string.h** header file in your program to use these functions.

The following are the most commonly used string handling functions.

Method	Description
strcat()	It is used to concatenate(combine) two string
strlen()	It is used to show length of a string
strrev()	It is used to show reverse of a string
strcpy()	Copies one string into another
strcmp()	It is used to compare two string

strcat() function: strcat() function will add the string
Example: strcat("GPT", "Gadag");
strcat() function will add the string **"Gadag"** to **"GPT"**.

strlen() function: strlen() function will return the length of the string passed to it.

Example:

```
int j;
j=strlen("vittalkumar");
printf("%d",j);
```

output : 11

strcmp() function: strcmp() function will return the ASCII difference between first unmatching character of two strings.

Example:

```
int j;
j=strcmp("sun","moon");
printf("%d",j);
```

output:

```
-1
```

3.3 Introduction to Pointers

Pointers are variables that hold address of another variable of same data type. Pointers are one of the most distinct and exciting features of C language. It provides power and flexibility to the language. Although pointer may appear little confusing and complicated in the beginning, but it is a powerful tool and handy to use once it is mastered.

3.3.1 Benefit of using Pointers

- ☞ Pointers are more efficient in handling Array and Structure.
- ☞ Pointer allows references to function and thereby helps in passing of function as arguments to other function.
- ☞ It reduces length and the program execution time.
- ☞ It allows C to support dynamic memory management.

3.3.2 Concept of Pointer

Whenever a **variable** is declared, system will allocate a location to that variable in the memory, to hold value. This location will have its own address number.

Let us assume that system has allocated memory location 80F for a variable **a**.

```
int a = 10 ;
```

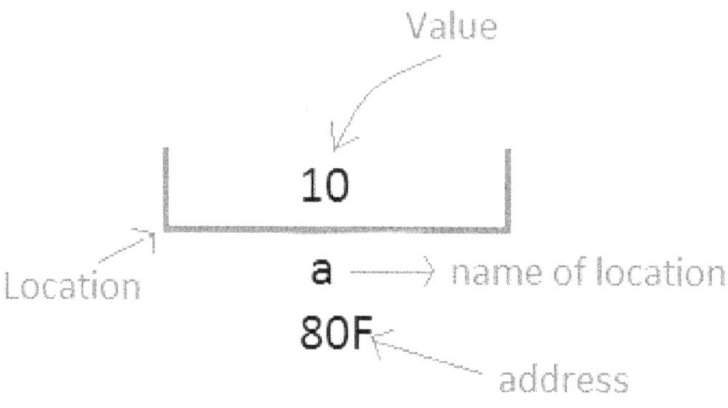

We can access the value 10 by either using the variable name "**a**" or the address 80F. Since the memory addresses are simply numbers they can be assigned to some other variable. The variable that holds memory address is called pointer variable.

Hence a pointer variable is therefore nothing but a variable that contains an address, which is a location of another variable. Value of pointer variable will be stored in another memory location.

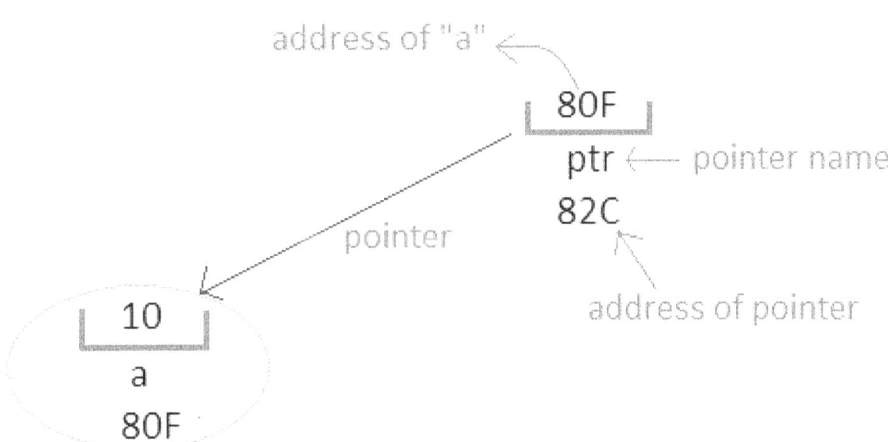

3.3.3 Declaring a Pointer Variable

General syntax of pointer declaration is,

```
data-type *pointer_name;
```

Data type of pointer must be same as the variable, which the pointer is pointing. **void** type pointer works with all data types, but isn't used often.

3.3.4 Initialization of Pointer Variable

Pointer initialization is the process of assigning address of a variable to pointer variable. Pointer variable contains address of variable of same data type. In C language address operator "&" is used to determine the address of a variable. The "&" (immediately preceding a variable name) returns the address of the variable associated with it.

```
int  a = 10 ;
int *ptr ;          //pointer declaration
ptr = &a ;          //pointer initialization
or,
int *ptr = &a ;        //initialization and declaration together
```

Pointer variable always points to same type of data.

```
float a;
int *ptr;
ptr = &a;      //ERROR, type mismatch
```

Chapter 4

Functions

4.1 Functions in c

In C programming, a function is a segment that groups code to perform a specific task. A C program has at least one function main(). Without main() function, there is technically no C program.

4.1.1 Benefits of Functions

- ☞ User defined functions helps to decompose the large program into small segments which makes programmer easy to understand, maintain and debug.
- ☞ If repeated code occurs in a program. Function can be used to include those codes and execute when needed by calling that function.
- ☞ Programmer working on large project can divide the workload by making different functions.

4.1.2 C Function Definition, Function Declaration and Function Call

Function definition: This contains all the statements to be executed. Its syntax is as below

```
return_type function_name ( arguments list )
{ Body of function; }
```

Function declaration or prototype: This informs compiler about the function name, function parameters and return value's data type. Its syntax is as below

```
return_type function_name ( argument list );
```

Function call: This calls the actual function. Its syntax is as below

```
function_name ( arguments list );
```

4.2 Types of C functions

There are two types of functions in C programming:

☞ Library function
☞ User defined function

4.2.1 Library function

Library functions are the in-built function in C programming system. For example:

main(): The execution of every C program starts from this main() function.

printf(): prinf() is used for displaying output in C.

scanf(): scanf() is used for taking input in C.

4.2.2 User defined function

C allows programmer to define their own function according to their requirement. These types of functions are known as user-defined functions.

Suppose a programmer wants to find factorial of a number and check whether it is prime or not in same program. Then, he/she can create two separate user-defined functions in that program: one for finding factorial and other for checking whether it is prime or not. And these two are called in main program

4.2.3 How user-defined function works in C Programming?

```
#include <stdio.h>
void function_name(){
        ................
        ................
}

int main() {
        ...........
        ...........          step 1
        function_name();
        ...........
        ...........
}
```

step 2

Fig: Working of Functions

As mentioned earlier, every C program begins from main() and program starts executing the codes inside main() function. When the control of program reaches to function_name() inside main() function. The control of program jumps to void function_name() and executes the codes inside it. When all the codes inside that user-defined function are executed, control of the program jumps to the statement just after function_name() from where it is called.

4.3 Calling C functions/Parameter Passing

There are two ways that a C function can be called from a program. They are,

☞ Call by value/ Pass by value
☞ Call by reference/Pass by address

4.3.1 Call by Value

☞ In call by value method, the value of the variable is passed to the function as parameter.
☞ The value of the actual parameter cannot be modified by formal parameter.
☞ Different memory is allocated for both actual and formal parameters because value of actual parameter is copied to formal parameter.

Note:

☞ Actual parameter – This is the argument which is used in function call.
☞ Formal parameter – This is the argument which is used in function definition

Example: C program to swap using call by value function.

```c
#include<stdio.h>
void swap (int a, int b);   // function prototype, also called function declaration
int main()
{
    int m = 22, n = 44;    // calling swap function by value
    printf(" values before swap  m = %d \n and n = %d", m, n);
    swap(m, n);
}
void swap(int a, int b)
{
    int tmp;
    tmp = a;
    a =  b;
    b = temp;
printf(" values after swap  m = %d \n and n = %d", a, b);
}

Output:
values before swap m = 22 and n = 44
values after swap m = 44 and n = 22
```

4.3.2 Call by reference:

☞ In call by reference method, the address of the variable is passed to the function as parameter.
☞ The value of the actual parameter can be modified by formal parameter.
☞ Same memory is used for both actual and formal parameters since only address is used by both parameters.

Example: C program to swap using call by reference function.

```c
#include<stdio.h>
void swap(int *a, int *b);       // function prototype, also called function declaration
```

```c
int main()
{
    int m = 22, n = 44;
    //  calling swap function by reference
    printf("values before swap m = %d \n and n = %d",m,n);
    swap(&m, &n);
}

void swap(int *a, int *b)
{
    int tmp;
    tmp = *a;
    *a = *b;
    *b = tmp;
    printf("\n values after swap a = %d \nand b = %d", *a, *b);
}
```

Output:
```
values before swap m = 22 and n = 44
values after swap m = 44 and n = 22
```

4.4 Recursive Function

A function that calls itself is known as recursive function and this technique is known as recursion in C programming.

Example: Write a C program to find sum of first n natural numbers using recursion. Note: Positive integers are known as natural number i.e. 1, 2, 3....n

```c
#include <stdio.h>
int sum(int n);
int main(){
    int num,add;
    printf("Enter a positive integer:\n");
    scanf("%d",&num);
    add=sum(num);
    printf("sum=%d",add);
}
int sum(int n){
    if(n==0)
        return n;
    else
        return n+sum(n-1);    /*self call  to function sum() */
}
```

Output
```
Enter a positive integer:
```

```
5
15
```

In, this simple C program, sum() function is invoked from the same function. If n is not equal to 0 then, the function calls itself passing argument 1 less than the previous argument it was called with. Suppose, n is 5 initially. Then, during next function calls, 4 is passed to function and the value of argument decreases by 1 in each recursive call. When, n becomes equal to 0, the value of n is returned which is the sum numbers from 5 to 1.

Every recursive function must be provided with a way to end the recursion. In this example when, n is equal to 0, there is no recursive call and recursion ends.

4.4.1 Advantages and Disadvantages of Recursion

Recursion is more elegant and requires few variables which make program clean. Recursion can be used to replace complex nesting code by dividing the problem into same problem of its sub-type.

In other hand, it is hard to think the logic of a recursive function. It is also difficult to debug the code containing recursion.

4.5 Data Visibility and Longevity

A scope in any programming is a region of the program where a defined variable can have its existence and beyond that variable it cannot be accessed. There are two places where variables can be declared in C programming language –

- ☞ Inside a function or a block which is called local variables.
- ☞ Outside of all functions which is called global variables.

4.5.1 Local Variables

Variables that are declared inside a function or block are called local variables. They can be used only by statements that are inside that function or block of code. Local variables are not known to functions outside their own.

4.5.2 Global Variables

Global variables are defined outside a function, usually on top of the program. Global variables hold their values throughout the lifetime of program and they can be accessed inside any of the functions defined for that program.

A global variable can be accessed by any function. That is, a global variable is available for use throughout your entire program after its declaration.

The following program show how global variables and local variables are used in a program.

```c
#include <stdio.h>
 int g;       /* global variable declaration */

int main () {
    int a, b;       /* local variable declaration */
  a = 10;     /* actual initialization */
  b = 20;
  g = a + b;
```

```
   printf ("value of a = %d, b = %d and g = %d\n", a, b, g);
   return 0;
}
```

A program can have same name for local and global variables but the value of local variable inside a function will take preference.

```
#include <stdio.h>
 int g = 20; /* global variable declaration */

int main () {
    int g = 10;                 /* local variable declaration */
  printf ("value of g = %d\n",  g);
    return 0;
}
```

When the above code is compiled and executed, it produces the following result –
value of g = 10

Chapter 5

User Defined Data Type

5.1 Introduction to Structure

Structure is a user-defined data type in C which allows you to combine different data types to store a particular type of record. Structure helps to construct a complex data type in more meaningful way. It is somewhat similar to an Array. The only difference is that array is used to store collection of similar datatypes while structure can store collection of any type of data.

Structure is used to represent a record. Suppose you want to store record of student which consists of student name, address, roll number and age. You can define a structure to hold this information.

5.1.1 Defining a Structure

"struct" keyword is used to define a structure. **struct** define a new data type which is a collection of different type of data.

Syntax:
```
struct structure_name
{
 //Statements
```

```
};
```

Example:
```
struct Book
{
 char name[15];
 int price;
 int pages;
};
```

Here the **struct Book** declares a structure to hold the details of book which consists of three data fields, namely name, price and pages. These fields are called **structure elements or members**. Each member can have different data type, like in this case, **name** is of char type and **price** is of int type etc. **Book** is the name of the structure and is called structure tag.

5.1.2 Declaring Structure Variables

It is possible to declare variables of a **structure**, once the structure is defined. **Structure** variable declaration is similar to the declaration of variables of any other data types. Structure variables can be declared in following two ways.

1) Declaring Structure variables separately
```
struct Student
{
 char[20] name;
 int age;
 int rollno;
} ;
```

```
struct Student S1 , S2;    //declaring variables of Student
```

2) Declaring Structure Variables with Structure definition
```
struct Student
{
 char[20] name;
 int age;
 int rollno;
} S1, S2 ;
```
Here **S1** and **S2** are variables of structure **Student**. However this approach is not much recommended.

5.1.3 Accessing Structure Members

Structure members can be accessed and assigned values in number of ways. Structure member has no meaning independently. In order to assign a value to a structure member, the member name must be linked with the structure variable using dot (.) operator also called period or member access operator.
```
struct Book
{
 char name[15];
```

```
  int price;
  int pages;
} b1 , b2 ;
```

b1.price=200;   //b1 is variable of Book type and price is member of Book

We can also use scanf() to give values to structure members through terminal.

```
scanf(" %s ", b1.name);
scanf(" %d ", &b1.price);
```

5.1.4 Structure Initialization

Like any other data type, structure variable can also be initialized at compile time.

Example:

```
struct Patient
{
 float height;
 int weight;
 int age;
};

struct Patient p1 = { 180.75 , 73, 23 };      //initialization
or,
struct patient p1;
p1.height = 180.75;      //initialization of each member separately
p1.weight = 73;
p1.age = 23;
```

5.1.5 Array of Structure

We can also declare an array of structure. Each element of the array representing a structure variable.

Example : struct employee emp[5];

The above code define an array emp of size 5 elements. Each element of array emp is of type employee

```
#include<stdio.h>
#include<conio.h>
struct employee
{
 char ename[10];
 int sal;
};

struct employee emp[5];
int i,j;
void ask()
{
 for(i=0;i<3;i++)
 {
```

```
 printf("\nEnter %dst employee record\n",i+1);
 printf("\nEmployee name\t");
 scanf("%s",emp[i].ename);
 printf("\nEnter employee salary\t");
 scanf("%d",&emp[i].sal);
 }
 printf("\nDisplaying Employee record\n");
 for(i=0;i<3;i++)
 {
 printf("\nEmployee name is %s",emp[i].ename);
 printf("\nSlary is %d",emp[i].sal);
 }
}
void main()
{
 clrscr();
 ask();
 getch();
}
```

5.2 Unions in C Language

Unions are conceptually similar to structures. The syntax of union is also similar to that of structure. The only difference is in terms of storage. In structure each member has its own storage location, whereas all members of union uses a single shared memory location which is equal to the size of its largest data member.

Example:

```
union item
{
 int m;
 float x;
 char c;
}It1;
```

This declares a variable It1 of type union item. This union contains three members each with a different data type. However only one of them can be used at a time. This is due to the fact that only one location is allocated for a union variable, irrespective of its size. The compiler allocates the storage that is large enough to hold largest variable type in the union. In the union declared above the member x requires 4 bytes which is largest among the members in 16-bit machine. Other members of union will share the same address.

5.2.1 Distinction between Structures and Unions

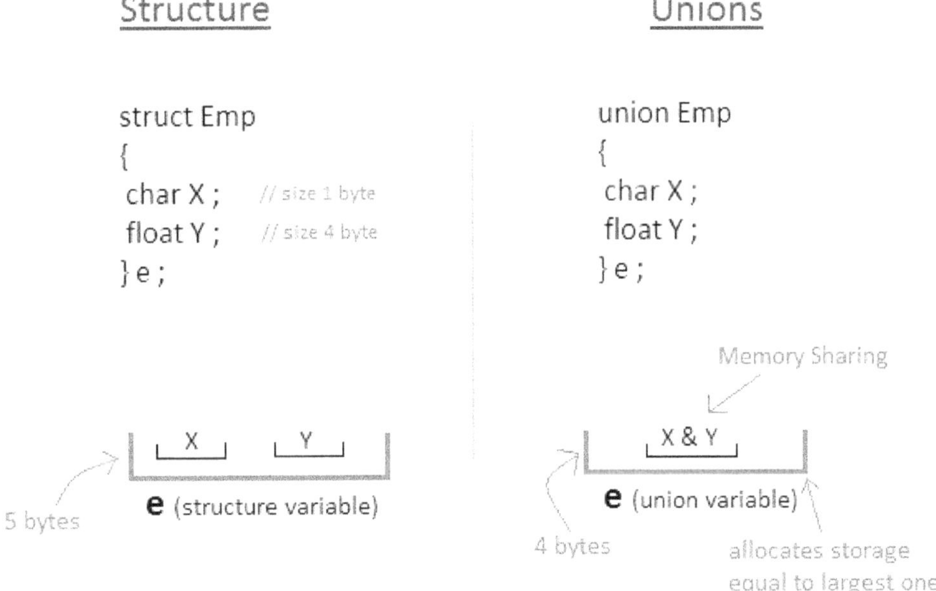

This implies that although a union may contain many members of different types, it cannot handle all the members at same time. A union is declared using union keyword.

5.2.2 Accessing a Union Member

Syntax for accessing union member is similar to accessing structure member,

```
union test
{
  int a;
  float b;
  char c;
}t;


t.a ;        //to access members of union t
t.b ;
t.c ;
```

Complete Example for Union

```
#include <stdio.h>
#include <conio.h>

union item
{
  int a;
  float b;
  char ch;
};

int main( )
```

```c
{
 union item it;
 it.a = 12;
 it.b = 20.2;
 it.ch='z';
 clrscr();
 printf("%d\n",it.a);
 printf("%f\n",it.b);
 printf("%c\n",it.ch);
 getch();
 return 0;
}
```

Output :
```
-26426
20.1999
z
```

As you can see here, the values of a and b get corrupted and only variable c prints the expected result. Because in union, the only member whose value is currently stored will have the memory.

Chapter 6

Macros

6.1 Definition of Macro

A macro is a name given to a block of C statements as a pre-processor directive. Being a pre-processor, the block of code is communicated to the compiler before entering into the actual coding (main () function). A macro is defined with the preprocessor directive, #define.

The advantage of using macro is the execution speed of the program fragment. When the actual code snippet is to be used, it can be substituted by the name of the macro. The same block of statements, on the other hand, need to be repeatedly hard coded as and when required.

The disadvantage of the macro is the size of the program. The reason is, the pre-processor will replace all the macros in the program by its real definition prior to the compilation process of the program.

6.2 Classification of Macros

Several object-like macros are predefined; you use them without supplying their definitions. They fall into three classifications as mentioned below

- ☞ Standard predefined macros
- ☞ Common predefined macros
- ☞ System-specific predefined macros

6.2.1 Standard Predefined Macros

The standard predefined macros are specified by the relevant language standards, so they are available with all compilers that implement those standards. Older compilers may not provide all of them. Their names all start with double underscores. Few of the standard predefined macros are as follows

_ _DATE_ _: String containing the current date

_ _FILE_ _: String containing the file name

_ _LINE_ _: Integer representing the current line number

_ _STDC_ _: If follows ANSI standard C, then value is a nonzero integer

_ _TIME_ _: String containing the current time.

6.2.2 Common Predefined Macros

The common predefined macros are GNU (Gernal name Unix but GNUs Not Unix) C extensions. They are available with the same meanings regardless of the machine or operating system on which you are using GNU C or GNU Fortran. Their names all start with double underscores. Few of the common predefined macros are as follows

_ _BASE_FILE_ _: This macro expands to the name of the main input file, in the form of a C string constant.

_ _INCLUDE_LEVEL_ _: This macro expands to a decimal integer constant that represents the depth of nesting in include files. The value of this macro is incremented on every '#include' directive and decremented at the end of every included file.

_ _ELF_ _: This macro is defined if the target uses the ELF object format.

_ _VERSION_ _: This macro expands to a string constant which describes the version of the compiler in use.

_ _COUNTER_ _: This macro expands to sequential integral values starting from 0.

6.2.3 System-Specific Predefined Macros

The C preprocessor normally predefines several macros that indicate what type of system and machine is in use. All system-specific predefined macros expand to a constant value, so you can test them with either '#ifdef' or '#if'.

The C standard requires that all system-specific macros be part of the reserved namespace. All names which begin with two underscores, or an underscore and a capital letter, are reserved for the compiler and library to use as they wish.

When the -ansi option, or any -std option that requests strict conformance, is given to the compiler, all the system-specific predefined macros outside the reserved namespace are suppressed. The parallel macros, inside the reserved namespace, remain defined.

#define: Use this to define constants or any macro substitution. Use as follows:

#define <macro> <replacement name>

For Example

        #define FALSE 0
        #define AGE 10

#undef: This commands <u>undefined</u> a macro. A macro must be undefined before being redefined to a different value.

#include: This directive includes a file into code.

It has two possible forms:

        #include <file>

 or

        #include "file"

#if -- Conditional inclusion: #if evaluates a constant integer expression. You <u>always</u> need a #endif to delimit end of statement.

        We can have else etc. as well by using #else and #elif -- else if.

Another common use of #if is with:

    #ifdef: if defined and

    #ifndef: if not defined

Example: C program to display current date using macro

```c
#include <stdio.h>
int main()
{
    printf("Current time: %s",__TIME__);    //calculate the current time
}
```
Output
```
Current time: 19:54:39
```

Example: C Program to find area of a circle using macro

```c
#include <stdio.h>
#define PI 3.1415
int main()
{
    int radius;
    float area;
    printf("Enter the radius: ");
    scanf("%d",&radius);
    area=PI*radius*radius;
    printf("Area=%.2f",area);
    return 0;
}
```
Output
```
Enter the radius: 3
Area=28.27
```